The U.S. Congress

by Patricia J. Murphy

Content Adviser: Kathleen M. Kendrick, Project Historian,
National Museum of American History, Smithsonian Institution

Social Science Adviser: Professor Sherry L. Field,
Department of Curriculum and Instruction,
College of Education, The University of Texas at Austin

Reading Adviser: Dr. Linda D. Labbo, Department of Reading Education,
College of Education, The University of Georgia

Let's See Library

Compass Point Books

Minneapolis, Minnesota

Compass Point Books
3109 West 50th Street, #115
Minneapolis, MN 55410

Visit Compass Point Books on the Internet at *www.compasspointbooks.com* or e-mail your
request to *custserv@compasspointbooks.com*

Photographs ©: Digital Stock, cover; Reuters NewMedia/Corbis, 4; Stock Montage, 6; North Wind Picture
Archives, 8 (all); Photo Network, 10; AP/Wide World, 12; AFP/Corbis, 14, 18 (all); Unicorn Stock Photos/Florent
Flipper, 16; Reuters/Peter Morgan/Hulton Getty/Archive Photos, 20.

Editors: E. Russell Primm, Emily J. Dolbear, Laura Driscoll, and Karen Commons
Photo Researchers: Svetlana Zhurkina and Jo Miller
Photo Selector: Linda S. Koutris
Designer: Melissa Voda

Library of Congress Cataloging-in-Publication Data
Murphy, Patricia J., 1963–
     The U.S. Congress / by Patricia J. Murphy.
        p. cm. — (Let's see library)
     Includes bibliographical references and index.
     ISBN 0-7565-0196-2 (hardcover)
     1. United States. Congress—Juvenile literature. [1. United States. Congress.] I. Title. I. Let's see library. Our
nation.
  JK1025 .M87 2002
  328.73—dc21   2001004483

Table of Contents

What Is the U.S. Congress?

The U.S. Congress is a part of our government. It is made up of people from each state. The members of Congress meet and make laws for our country.

The U.S. Congress has two parts. One part is called the U.S. Senate. The Senate has 100 members. Each member is called a **senator**.

The other part of Congress is the U.S. House of Representatives, or "the House." The House has 435 members. Each member is called a **representative**.

◄ *These members of the House of Representatives were sworn in on January 3, 2001.*

Who Created Congress?

A group of Americans called the "Founding Fathers" created the U.S. Congress. In 1787, they wrote a plan for our government.

They decided that the government should have three branches. One branch would make sure people follow the laws. Another branch would decide what the laws mean. A third branch would make the laws.

The part of our government that makes laws is called the **legislative branch**. The Founding Fathers made the U.S. Congress a part of this branch.

◄ *In 1787, the Founding Fathers made Congress a part of the new U.S. government.*

Why Does Congress Have Two Parts?

The Founding Fathers did not agree on everything. Some of them wanted Congress to have two members from each state. Others thought states with more people should have more members. The two sides talked it over and decided to have both!

In the Senate, there are two members from each state. In the House of Representatives, some states have only one representative. Other states have more than thirty. The more people a state has, the more representatives it has.

◄ *Founding Fathers Roger Sherman (top) and Oliver Ellsworth (bottom) thought that Congress should have two parts—a Senate and a House of Representatives.*

Where Does Congress Meet?

The U.S. Congress meets in the Capitol in Washington, D.C. The Senate meets in a room called the Senate Chamber. The House meets in another room called the House Chamber.

In the House and the Senate, members of Congress take turns speaking when they meet. They talk about making new laws. A member of Congress might speak for or against making new laws.

◄ *Members of Congress meet in the Capitol.*

When Does Congress Meet?

Most years, Congress meets between January 3 and July 31. It may meet later in the summer if it has work to finish.

The Senate and the House do not always meet on the same days. They also do not meet every day. They often meet in **committees**. Committees work on making new laws.

On some days, members of Congress go home to their states. They talk about issues. They find out how the people feel about ideas for new laws.

◀ *Rep. Luis Gutierrez of Illinois talks to people about issues that affect his district.*

How Does Congress Make Laws?

Written plans for new laws are called **bills**. Bills can start in the House or the Senate.

Let's say a senator has a bill. After the senator speaks for the bill, the Senate may vote on it. If most of the senators vote for the bill, it goes to the House. If most of the representatives vote for the bill, it goes to the president of the United States. The president must sign the bill before it becomes a law.

What about a bill that starts in the House? It is put to a vote in the House and then the Senate. Then the president must sign it.

◀ *President George W. Bush signs a bill into law.*

What Other Powers Does Congress Have?

The U.S. Congress decides how our country spends the government's money. It also has the power to print new money.

The Congress can declare war on another country. If the president breaks the law, the Congress can put him on trial.

The Senate can say yes or no to the people the president chooses for important jobs. The Senate must approve heads of government departments and justices of the Supreme Court.

◄ *Congress decides how much new money to print each year.*

Who Are the Leaders of Congress?

The leader of the House is called the Speaker of the House. He or she leads discussion when the House meets. A representative must ask the Speaker for permission to speak.

The leader of the Senate is the vice president of the United States. If there is a tie in the Senate, the vice president breaks it. However, the vice president does not come to the Senate often. When the vice president is not present, the leader of the Senate is the *president pro tempore*. That is Latin for "president for the time being."

◄ *Dennis Hastert (top left) was elected Speaker of the House in 1999. Robert Byrd (bottom) serves as the president pro tempore of the Senate.*

How Do People Become Members of Congress?

People vote for their members of Congress in elections. Senators and representatives must be U.S. citizens. They must live in the state they serve.

A senator must be at least thirty years old. He or she must have lived in the United States for nine years. A representative must be at least twenty-five years old. He or she must have lived in the United States for seven years.

Senators serve a **term** of six years. Representatives serve two-year terms. Members of Congress can run for office as many times as they want.

◄ *Barbara Boxer from California ran for election to the U.S. Senate in 1992. She won and was reelected in 1998.*

Glossary

bills—written plans for new laws

committees—groups of representatives or senators who meet to make decisions for the House or the Senate

legislative branch—the part of the U.S. government that makes laws

representative—a member of the U.S. House of Representatives

senator—a member of the U.S. Senate

term—the length of time for which a member of Congress is voted into office

Did You Know?

• The word *Congress* means "come together."

• You can suggest a bill. Write to your senator or representative if you have an idea for a new law.

• The Capitol has a barbershop, a subway, several dining rooms, and doctors' offices.

Want to Know More?

At the Library

Quiri, Patricia Ryon. *Congress.* Danbury, Conn.: Children's Press, 1999.
Stein, R. Conrad. *The Powers of Congress.* Chicago: Children's Press, 1995.
Weber, Michael. *Our Congress.* Brookfield, Conn.: Millbrook Press, 1994.

On the Web

For more information on this topic, use FactHound.

1. Go to *www.facthound.com*
2. Type in this book ID: 076501962
3. Click on the *Fetch It* button.
Facthound will find the best Web sites for you.

Through the Mail

The U.S. House of Representatives
c/o The Honorable [full name of your representative]
Washington, DC 20510
For answers to any questions you may have for your representative

On the Road

The U.S. Capitol
Capitol Hill
Washington, DC 20515
202/225-6827
To go on a free tour of the Capitol and to see members of Congress at work

Index

About the Author
Patricia J. Murphy writes children's storybooks, nonfiction books, early readers, and poetry. She also writes for magazines, corporations, educational publishing companies, and museums. She is the owner of PattyCake Productions and lives in Northbrook, Illinois.